The World of
Wild
Animals

Ton van Eerbeek

BALLOON BOOKS™

Where do gorillas sleep?

* On a bed made of branches.

GORILLA

Gorillas are the largest and most powerful apes. They live in groups in the rain forests of western Africa. They eat berries and fruit rind. They rarely drink water. Fruits supply the water that their bodies need.

KANGAROO

Young kangaroos
grow in a pouch on
their mothers' stomachs.
Kangaroos live in Australia and on
the island of Papua New Guinea. There are
60 different types of kangaroos. They all eat plants.

Do kangaroos move
by running or jumping?
* Jumping: One jump can be
up to 20 feet long.

What is a bottle nose?

* A type of dolphin.

DOLPHIN

Dolphins are intelligent mammals that live in the sea and eat fish. Their bodies are shaped like rockets, which allow them to swim fast. They like to follow boats so that they can play in their waves.

ORCA

The orca, or killer whale,
can be almost 30 feet long.
Orcas are actually in the dolphin family.
They are predators who hunt fish, sea lions,
penguins, and squid. They catch their prey by
sending out sounds, which echo and are then received.

How many teeth do orcas have?

* They have 40 to 50 razor-sharp teeth.

Are foxes very clever?

* Yes. In the city, they take leftovers out of garbage cans.

FOX

Foxes are found in almost every part of the world. They live in forests, heaths, and prairies. During the day, they sleep in a den; at night, they look for food. They catch rabbits and mice, but also enjoy insects and berries.

WOLF

Wolves can grow to be almost 2 ½ feet long. They are in the dog family. Wolves live in the forests and mountains of North America, northern Europe, and Siberia. They form into groups of 10 to 20 and hunt bison and reindeer.

How long do male and female wolves stay together?

* Their entire lives.

How fast can a brown bear run?

* It can run 30 miles per hour.

BROWN BEAR

Brown bears are commonly seen in forests in the United States and Canada. They can be 7 ½ feet tall. They eat everything they find: plants and animals. In the winter, females give birth to two to three bear cubs.

POLAR BEAR

Gigantic polar bears are easy
to recognize because of their white fur,
which acts as a camouflage. A male polar bear can
be 7 ½ feet tall and weigh up to 1,325 pounds. Females
give birth to two to four polar bear cubs each year. Polar
bears catch fish and seals, but they love eating berries.

*In the cold North Pole region.

Where do polar bears live?

Did you know that all kittens are born blind?

WILD CAT

Wild cats look very much like house cats. Wild cats are in the cat family. Wild cats live in forests, open grasslands, and the warm regions of Europe, Africa, and Asia. They hunt mice and birds. Females give birth to two to four kittens.

LEOPARD

Leopards are also
called panthers. These
feline predators live in the forests,
deserts, and mountains in Africa and
Asia. Leopards hunt large animals, such as
antelopes and deer; but also like snakes, apes, and fish.

Did you know that leopards are able to pull a large prey up in a tree so that they can slowly eat it?

Did you know that tiger cubs stay with their mother until they are three years old?

TIGER

With a length of almost 10 ½ feet, tigers are the largest feline predators. There are eight different types of tigers. The Bengal and Siberian tigers are the most well-known. Tigers are forest dwellers. They hunt alone and catch mostly deer.

LION

Lions are lazy animals.
They sleep 20 hours a day!
These large cats, which live in
Africa and India, have no natural
enemies. Females, called lionesses, form groups
and hunt large animals, such as zebras and antelopes.

Why do lions roar?

* To let other lions hear where their territory, or living area, is located.

Why do zebras
have stripes?

* To confuse predators.

ZEBRA

Zebras are part of the horse family. There are three kinds of zebras. They live in large herds on grassland in the warm parts of Africa. This means that their food consists almost entirely of grass. The females are called mares and baby zebras are called foals.

ELEPHANT

There are
two kinds of elephants.
The African (pictured here) has
large, protruding ears; the Asiatic
has small ears. A male African elephant can
weigh 6 tons. They eat leaves, twigs, and fruit.

What do elephants use their trunks for?

* To bring food and water to their mouths.

Did you know that a rhinoceros has very poor vision, but a good sense of smell and good hearing?

RHINOCEROS

The five types of rhinoceros (two in Africa and three in Asia) were hunted for their horns; therefore, they are now very rare. The front horn of the African black rhinoceros can be 4 feet long. Rhinoceros are plant eaters: they mainly eat grass.

HIPPOPOTAMUS

Hippopotamuses live in herds
in Africa. During the day, they lie in
the water; in the evening, they come on land
to eat grass and fruit. They like to fight. They open their
enormous mouths wide and roar loudly before they attack.
Male hippopotamuses can seriously wound one another.

Did you know that hippopotamuses can "run" over river bottoms under water?

Do you know how giraffes fight one another?

* They "hit" each other with their long necks.

GIRAFFE

A giraffe's head can hang 19 ½ feet above the ground because of their very long necks. Short horns sprout from their heads. Giraffes live on grasslands in Africa. They eat leaves and twigs, which they pluck from trees with their tongues.

BISON

Did you know that Native Americans once used every part of a bison's body to survive?

At one time, millions of bison lived on the North American grasslands, which are called prairies. Around 1900, they were almost extinct due to over-hunting. Fortunately, laws were made to protect the bison from becoming extinct. Bison weigh almost 2,000 pounds.

The nest of the North American sea eagle can be up to 16 feet across!

EAGLE

Eagles are large birds of prey.
There are 25 kinds of eagles.
The Bald Eagle is now protected.
Eagles ate too many poisoned fish
over the years and became endangered. Thankfully,
their numbers are growing more and more each year!

PENGUIN

Penguins shoot through
the water when they hunt
for fish. Their wings serve as
paddles. On land, penguins walk upright.
Penguins huddle into packs to conserve heat.
None of the 17 types of penguins can fly.

How fast can penguins swim?

* They can swim about 25 miles per hour.

Did you know that mother crocodiles guard their nests of 20 to 30 eggs for three months?

CROCODILE

Crocodiles are reptiles. Therefore, they are cold-blooded and must warm their bodies in the sun. Crocodiles can be up to 22 ½ feet long. They like to eat deer and other animals. Crocodiles almost became extinct due to over-hunting.

TURTLE

There are land turtles
(see photo) and water turtles.
Water turtles are good swimmers.
These reptiles protect their soft body
parts with a hard shell. Snails are one of their
favorite foods. Females bury their eggs in the sand.

How long have turtles existed on earth?
* 200 million years!

Index

Source of the illustrations:
Photographs by HR Tierfoto and Diapress